THE EXPERIENCE OF POETRY

BY THE SAME AUTHOR

Prose

The Street of Queer Houses
Beads of Coloured Days
Here and Otherwhere
Silver Nutmegs
Pitiful Dust
Eternity in an Hour

Verse

Poems
The Ripening Years
Prince Jonathan

THE EXPERIENCE
OF POETRY

BY
VERNON KNOWLES

LONDON
GEORGE NEWNES LIMITED

Is this enjoyment of poetry, this delight in beauty, rare or common? It is both: as a settled habit it is rare . . .; it is common, as the native tendency of all ingenuous minds—BENEDETTO CROCE.

Printed in Great Britain by Wyman & Sons Ltd.,
London, Reading and Fakenham

CONTENTS

THE EXPERIENCE OF POETRY

CHAPTER I

THE FEAR OF POETRY

§

THERE is one main reason why the plain man (whom we have all met) dislikes poetry and avoids it entirely in his reading.

It is Fear.

" Poetry ! " he exclaims—and recalls, with inward shuddering, the verses he was forced to learn by heart in his schooldays. Jingling, obscure things, they merely tormented him, taught him nothing, and gave him the reverse of delight.

A shadow, instead of a radiance, fell across his path.

*　　　*　　　*　　　*

He is a plain man, he will declare

immodestly, and poetry is " over his head."
It deals with abstractions and highfalutin
themes that soar beyond the commonplaces
that fill, and are, his life. He has not the
time to unravel their intricacies ; nor,
indeed, the power to do so : poetry is
" highbrow," and therefore a thing esoteric,
out of his sphere. He will even go so far
as the elder Mr. Weller, and declare it to
be " unnat'ral." . . .

*   *   *   *

He inherits, unquestioningly, the tradi-
tion that poetry is hardly respectable.

His mind is filled with definite prejudices.
There was Oscar Wilde, he recalls vaguely,
and all that nonsense about green carnations
and blue china. Wilde wrote poetry, and
so did other weedy, long-haired men whose
morals were either exceedingly doubtful or
shamelessly non-existent.

He remembers, with satisfaction, that in
the late nineties of the last century and
in the first decade of this the mortality
of poets was gratifyingly high : drink and
suicide, between them, sharing the honours
of decimation.

Therefore, he argues, to read poetry is

to countenance its writers—those irresponsible, imponderable fellows—and thus to fail lamentably in the first duty of citizenship.

*   *   *   *

Perhaps the chiefest ingredient of his fear of poetry is the knowledge that it is flagrantly emotional.

Being emotional, it is therefore un-English—and to be shunned.

*   *   *   *

And although it is part of his creed that he can serve both God and Mammon honestly and sincerely, he emphatically denies the possibility of serving poetry and cricket-football-golf-and-business.

§

" Fear," says Alexander Cruden, " is a passion, implanted in nature, that causes a flight from an approaching evil, either real or imaginary." With our plain man, the fear of poetry is, of course, quite imaginary ; and—as in the best psycho-analytical circles

—when it is dissected and explained to him, it will be dispelled.

To begin with the first of his objections : He is quite right to shudder over the verses he learned at school. He is probably recalling

> It was a Summer evening,
>   Old Kaspar's work was done,
> And he before his cottage door
>   Was sitting in the sun.

Or else

> The shades of night were falling fast
> When through an Alpine village passed
> A youth who bore 'mid snow and ice
> A banner with the strange device,
>   Excelsior !

He will be puzzled to learn that these lines are *not* poetry. They are merely verse of a low order : each is an attempt at poetry that has failed.

The difference between poetry and verse is the difference between, say, two dry-cell batteries alike in appearance, but one charged with electricity, the other " dead."

For far too long have school-teachers marshalled all the rag, tag and bobtail of fifth-rate verse under the splendid banner of

Poetry, and fobbed off the miserable procession on innumerable young, uncritical minds.

But excuse for the boy is not excuse for the man. One has to unlearn many things one is taught at school, and " poetry " is one of them. Our plain man must turn a deaf ear to " It was a summer evening " and " The shades of night were falling fast," and the like, and prepare for something totally different, something wholly captivating—in fact, a New Experience.

    *   *   *   *

He will not think poetry " difficult " or " over his head " if he will only begin reading it with patience and common-sense.

All games have rules that must be mastered before they can be properly appreciated. Poetry has its rules, too. Patience and common-sense will assimilate them with ease.

Poetry, by its very nature, is terse rather than discursive, as is the tendency of prose ; each line is packed to its capacity ; each word—as each horse in a team—pulling its utmost weight.

The subject-matter covers the whole experience of man. It deals with the fundamentals and ultimates of existence : the things by which a man lives, and dies.

As such, it is as important as politics.

*   *   *   *

The popular notion that poetry is somewhat disreputable is, like most popular notions, laughably erroneous.

It became current in the first years of the present century, and owes its origin to the fact that a small band of minor poets—Oscar Wilde, Ernest Dowson, Lionel Johnson, Stephen Phillips, John Davidson —came to unfortunate ends soon after they had caught the public ear. They trailed the pageant of their bleeding heart before their small, precious audience with an ostentation begotten of rank exhibitionism. They were poseurs, in the main : world-weary, disillusioned, and very *fin de siècle*. However, they are not characteristic of the long line of English poets, nor is their work of any notable importance. They are rather oddities than portents, and against their unpleasant idiosyncrasies may be set the solid virtues of the genuine poets of their century : Tennyson, Browning and Matthew Arnold.

*   *   *   *

The bold, all-barriers-down emotionalism of poetry need not dismay. Our plain man will remember—after a moment's thought —the rapt enthusiasm he looses at a Cup-Tie game or a Test Match, and cease to urge this objection.

He will come, at length, to make the discovery that poetry, far from being a thing apart from his daily pursuits, is already inherent in them. Attempting to flee from poetry, he will find himself encompassed by it on all sides.

CHAPTER II

FROM THE BEGINNING

§

IT is not too much to say that the child is born to poetry as the sparks fly upward. He shows his appreciation of rhythm literally in his cradle and in his mother's arms : he coos with pleasure at the to-and-fro rockings ; he is soothed by them, and by their means is drawn into slumber. Is not the first gift to a child a rattle ? Watch how he beats it in the air, laughing with delight at the tintinnabulation. Later, watch how at meals he drums with his spoon on the table : bang-bang-banging with vigour and decision. And when he begins to lisp, he does so inevitably in numbers : his mother is "ma-ma," his father "da-da," and so he goes riming gaily on to "bow-wow," "puff-puff," and the like. What Milton calls

" the jingling sound of like endings " completely and unquestionably captivates him. He loves the dreamy indolence of a swing, the sharp staccato of a see-saw—entranced by the smooth fall and rise of the ground beneath him. Hearing music, he will sway this way and that in perfect accord with it.

But these things are mere steps to the threshold; with the discovery of Nursery Rimes he enters at once into the kingdom of poetry, where there are many mansions.

*   *   *   *

The child's initial experience of the world is through the first books that are read aloud to him. Without stirring from the nursery he is introduced to the gamut of human emotions. Later, he will be eager to fare forth and experience them at first-hand. But now, in his infancy and childhood, he is content to assimilate them passively, and form a conception—however distorted and open to correction upon correction—of the teeming world around, of which he is so amazingly a part. It was never prose that first charmed or excited him! No; prose lacks the essential qualities of conciseness and memorableness. It was verse,—and the verse was of course the traditional collection of Nursery Rimes.

With " Old Mother Hubbard " he makes acquaintance with the pathos of penury and want. For the rest of his life an empty cupboard will remain the unforgotten symbol of hunger and lack of pence.

He will have tears for " Who Killed Cock Robin ? " and the dirge will have the practical result of inculcating in him an awareness and regard not only for robins but for all birds ; indeed, for all dumb creatures. He will be sympathetic with " Little Bo-Peep " in her troubles, and share in " Old King Cole's " expansive jollity.

And, so far—hearing, absorbing and repeating these rimes—he is among things, persons and emotions familiar and recogniz-able : all the paraphernalia of everyday life. But as he goes on he makes acquaint-ance with another life, a gay, strange life that is lived in an incredible, extra-terrestrial world—the world of fantasy and grotesquerie. There, nothing is familiar ; magics and enchantments abound ; animals talk ; humans take on unguessable disguises ; there are romantic quests, impossible adventures, and invariably it is the unexpected, the improbable, that happens.

> Hey, diddle, diddle, the cat and the fiddle,
> The cow jumped over the moon ;
> The little dog laughed to see such sport,
> And the dish ran away with the spoon——

such are the commonplace happenings in this light-hearted world. A crooked man who lives with a crooked cat in a crooked house is one of its ordinary inhabitants, and so is an old woman who chooses, as a matter of course, to live with her large family in a shoe.

But at this point some of the rimes begin to give a deeper note. Let us say that they *all* are romantic, but the deeper note sounds when the romance becomes suddenly and astonishingly alert with beauty. The Little Boy Blues and the Little Miss Muffetts cease their jingling and slip away into the background, and the new measure takes the silence :

> Gray goose and gander,
> Waft your wings together,
> And carry the good King's daughter
> Over the one strand river.

B

It is the authentic voice of Poetry. Listen again :

> I had a little nut tree,
> Nothing would it bear
> But a silver nutmeg
> And a golden pear.
> The King of Spain's daughter
> Came to visit me—
> And all because
> Of my little nut tree.

And so, as it seems to me, this first book of the child's reading satisfies at once his clamorous, aboriginal poetic urge.

The things described, the events depicted, the emotions aroused, from the moment that they are assimilated become the basis of his future life. For a long time to come— if indeed they are ever eradicated at all, which is a moot question—consciously or unconsciously they remain the touchstone whereby all personal occurrences, all visiting emotions crowding in upon him in his hourly explorations, are tested. Later, they may sink into his subconscious mind, but even so their use and efficacy will remain unimpaired.

§

The incorrigible Max has remarked in an essay that it is one of the chief functions of a public school to take all the nonsense out of a boy, and of a university gently to put it all back again. But it seems that. with the child and poetry, with school the divine nonsense, the " bacchic fury " is rudely and effectively enough torn from him, but, university following or not, it is seldom if ever put back again. He is robbed of his birthright ; he is told he must begin to be " practical " and " sensible " ; that he is growing up now and must face " facts " ; that life is real and life is earnest —shibboleths shallow and ignorant. Truly, " shades of the prison-house begin to close upon the growing boy ! "

If he listens and becomes convinced and forgoes his birthright without further thought—his loss through the rest of his life is irreparable. At the core of his consciousness will gnaw a sense of something lacking, something vague but intensely real and desirable. He will go searching for it down all the ways of the world with blurred vision and stumbling steps. He is like Plato's divided human, ever searching for his counterpart, longing to be a *complete* person. If he finally comes up to it, winning at last to the unconjectured goal,—fortunate man ! his long loss is made good ; he is a completed being ; that which he denied does not in turn deny him : he is free henceforth of the kingdom of poetry and all its treasure.

CHAPTER III

THE MAN HIMSELF

§

OF the four main kinds of poetry, Lyrical, Dramatic, Narrative and Epic, by far the commonest and most popular is Lyrical.

All poets are singers, more or less, and the purely lyrical poet is the one possessed in the greatest degree of the quality and impulse of song. He is the natural egoist : concerned entirely with the world of himself—his thoughts and emotions. Sir Edward Dyer summed him up in the sixteenth century :

> My mind to me a kingdom is,
> Such present joys therein I find,
> That it excels all other bliss
> That earth affords or grows by kind.

The life that flows around him he regards only in as much as it impinges upon himself ; his writings, therefore, are strictly personal. They are also, by the same token, thoroughly biased ; it is not to the lyric poets that we go for impartiality and universality.

Since all human beings have in common the same emotions, it may be said that the lyric poet in giving expression to his feelings speaks for his inarticulate fellows. He interprets them to themselves. They are dumb, and he gives them a voice. From the dangerous anguish of pent-up emotion, he delivers them, and leads them on to knowledge of themselves.

In this office, lies his supreme value.

ON LOVE

Possessed of a hundred forms, the lyric is generally brief. It may be an ejaculation of joy, of sorrow, of fear, of aspiration ; it may capture a fleeting mood, or depict some part of the external world. But whatever its subject, it is always a personal statement, an intimate confession. *It is the man himself speaking.*

Perhaps it is inevitable that love should be the subject which occupies the forefront of the lyrist's attention. All the fears, fancies, hopes, jealousies and ardours of the lover—open the anthology where you will : on almost every page the perennial pre-occupation with " the first instinctive passion " is plain through the centuries. All the notes are rung that lie between delicacy and violence, between faith and black despair.

That nest of singing-birds, the minor Elizabethans, were so engaged in living intensely that they put all their passion into that gay adventure, and had little left over for their verses. What they did write, however, has charm, if superficiality, mellifluous numbers, if little weighty content. Sweet, airy little ditties, they are graceful swallow-dippings over the sea of love. They are content to describe the beloved, as for example Lodge's " Rosaline " :

> Like to the clear in highest sphere
>   Where all imperial glory shines,
> Of self-same colour is her hair. . . .
>
> Her eyes are sapphires set in snow. . . .
>
> Her eyes are like the blushing cloud
>   That beautifies Aurora's face. . . .

Her lips are like two budded roses
  Whom ranks of lilies neighbour nigh. . . .

Her neck like to a stately tower
  Where Love himself imprisoned lies. . . .

—and so on to the would-be wistful conclusion :

Then muse not, Nymphs, tho' I bemoan
  The absence of fair Rosaline,
Since for a fair there's fairer none,
  Nor for her virtues so divine :
    Heigh ho, fair Rosaline !
  Heigh ho, my heart ! would God that she were
    mine !

The easy comparisons lightly tripping
along, the final Heigh ho's, shew the poet's
facile and idly-harboured emotion. He is
not too serious ; it is only a passing fancy
after all ; half a sigh and Rosaline is quite
forgotten.

Campion's delightful " Cherry Ripe " is
in the same sort :

There is a garden in her face
  Where roses and white lilies blow ;
A heavenly paradise is that place,
  Wherein all pleasant fruits do flow :
There cherries grow which none may buy
Till " Cherry Ripe " themselves do cry.

—and Henry Wotton's wholly lovely

You meaner beauties of the night,
  That poorly satisfy our eyes

More by your number than your light,
    You common people of the skies ;
What are you when the moon shall rise ?

The note, though a little deeper, is still
the note of fancy. One cannot believe in
these quick, glancing songs : they delight
the ear but leave the heart untouched.

Marlowe's " passionate " shepherd pleads

Come live with me and be my love—

but offers nothing more substantial as an
inducement than that he will make her

beds of roses
    And a thousand fragrant posies ;
A cap of flowers and a kirtle
    Embroider'd all with leaves of myrtle.

A gown made of the finest wool
    Which from our pretty lambs we pull ;
Fair-lined slippers for the cold,
    With buckles of the purest gold.

A belt of straw and ivy-buds
    With coral clasps and amber studs :
And if these pleasures may thee move,
    Come live with me and be my Love.

Love, then, is a pleasant diversion, a
momentary amusement, a game over which
they pretend to break their hearts—" Ah,

were she pitiful as she is fair ! ''—and then
pass on to some other, and kinder, mistress :

> I loved thee once ;   I'll love no more ;

they are quite determined :   they'll

> go no more
> A-begging at a beggar's door.

George Wither speaks for them all in
typical light-heartedness :

> I loved a lass, a fair one,
>   As fair as e'er was seen ;
> She was indeed a rare one,
>   Another Sheba queen :
> But fool as then I was,
>   I thought she loved me too :
> But now, alas ! she's left me,
>   Falero, lero, loo !

—and in another poem, he demands :

> Shall I, wasting in despair,
> Die because a woman's fair ?

and it is obvious that, since he can reason
and debate the question so glibly, his feeling is lacking in the depth that leads on
to a relinquishing of life and all its joys.

Suckling is quite candid about the whole
matter ;   he comes smilingly out into the
open ;   no pretence here of broken heart
and sundered life ;   Love is a game indeed,
jolly and entertaining—but no more :

Out upon it, I have loved
  Three whole days together !
And am like to love three more,
  If it prove fair weather.

He knows all the rules, all the moves, and all the shifts :

Why so pale and wan, fond lover ?
  Prithee, why so pale ?
Will, when looking well can't move her,
  Looking ill prevail ?
  Prithee, why so pale ?

Why so dull and mute, young sinner ?
  Prithee, why so mute ?
Will, when speaking well can't win her,
  Saying nothing do't ?
  Prithee, why so mute ?

Quit, quit for shame !   This will not move ;
  This cannot take her.
If of herself she will not love,
  Nothing can make her :
  The devil take her !

Leaving the Elizabethans, who gallanted it through their short lives with their blithe hearts on their sleeves, we find the poets beginning to treat love more seriously. Banished are the posturing shepherds and the sparkling conceits ; a new sincerity is heard. Webbe's " Against Indifference " is a cry from the heart :

More love or more disdain I crave,
    Sweet, be not still indifferent :
O send me quickly to the grave,
    Or else afford me more content !
Or love or hate me more or less,
For love abhors all lukewarmness.

Give me a tempest if 'twill drive
    Me to the place where I would be ;
Or if you'll have me still alive,
    Confess you will be kind to me.
Give hopes of bliss or dig my grave :
More love or more disdain I crave.

And, more poignantly, Burns laments his dead Mary :

Thou ling'ring star, with less'ning ray,
    That lov'st to greet the early morn,
Again thou ush'rst in the day
    My Mary from my soul was torn.
O Mary ! dear departed shade !
    Where is thy place of blissful rest ?
Seest thou thy lover lowly laid ?
    Hear'st thou the groans that rend his breast ?

The loss of the beloved was never stated so simply nor so powerfully as by Wordsworth :

She lived unknown, and few could know
    When Lucy ceased to be ;
But she is in her grave, and, oh,
    The difference to me !

The direct and ordinary words of everyday use have taken on here a new dignity, achieved a sudden starkness that produces an effect of overwhelming pathos.

We are travelled far now from the Corinnas and Phillidas and their transparent semblances of passion. Love has become appreciated to the full of his majesty and just stature, as we see when Coleridge proclaims solemnly :

> All thoughts, all passions, all delights,
> Whatever stirs this mortal frame,
> All are but ministers of Love,
>   And feed his sacred flame.

There seems a reverential hush shadowed gravely behind the words of Byron's

> She walks in beauty, like the night
> Of cloudless climes and starry skies ;

—a hush that is born of beauty and remoteness—the twin attributes of love. But Browning fills all silence with the magnificence of his ringing cry of affirmation :

> O lyric love, half angel and half bird
> And all a wonder and a wild desire !

—lines whose adoring rapture we shall search in vain through the whole of our literature to match.

§

With the coming of the Victorian Era
the Muse's preoccupation with Venus seems
to have settled down somewhat and become domesticated. The note was first
set by a small lyric embedded in " The
Princess " of Tennyson :

> As thro' the land at eve we went,
>   And pluck'd the ripen'd ears,
> We fell out, my wife and I,
> O we fell out I know not why,
>   And kissed again with tears.
> And blessings on the falling out
>   That all the more endears,
> When we fall out with those we love
>   And kiss again with tears !
> For when we came where lies the child
>   We lost in other years,
> There above the little grave,
> O there above the little grave,
>   We kiss'd again with tears.

An unpretentious little lyric, verging upon,
if not actually crossing the threshold of,
mawkish sentimentality. It might serve—
and, indeed, *has* served times out of
number—as a scenario of one of Holly-
wood's less considerable productions. But
Tennyson could strike the resonant gong of
passion when he wished—as in "Fatima":

> O love, O fire, once he drew
> With one long kiss my whole soul thro'
> My lips, as sunlight drinketh dew ;

which, as a statement of the sheer physical anguish and ecstasy of love, we shall find only equalled, perhaps, in Rossetti.

And again, in another of "The Princess's" lyrics, "Summer Night"—the lines are quiet, but it is the quiet of intensity and desire :

> Now folds the lily all her sweetness up,
> And slips into the bosom of the lake :
> So fold thyself, my dearest, thou, and slip
> Into my bosom and be lost in me.

Notice there the insistence of the repetitive "thou" in the third line.

Matthew Arnold, beset by the transience of things, and seeking ever the Eternal amidst the flux ; usually so considered and collected in his statement, could rise to passion too on occasion. In "Dover Beach" he speaks of love—the highest love ; a mating of spirit with spirit—and, achingly aware of his mortal loneliness, reaches out to that single seeming-permanence :

Ah, love, let us be true
To one another ! for the world which seems

To lie before us like a land of dreams,
So various, so beautiful, so new,
Hath really neither joy, nor love, nor light,
Nor certitude, nor peace, nor help for pain ;
And we are here as on a darkling plain
Swept with confused alarms of struggle and flight,
Where ignorant armies clash by night.

Nowhere else in his poetry do we hear that strain again, so piteous and extreme.

But, these evidences of authentic passion apart, the Victorian domestication of love was proceeding apace, and in Coventry Patmore reached its apogee. His " Angel in the House," an account in a series of lyrics of fortunate nuptial love, though purposely of a studied simplicity, direct and unadorned, is a bald and unexciting recital. Competently, eloquently written, it is in effect pedestrian : a notable descent from the heights of passion.

Why, having won her, do I woo ?

he asks in the section entitled " The Married Lover," and answers :

Because her spirit's vestal grace
Provokes me always to pursue,
But, spirit-like, eludes embrace :

. . . because, in short,
She's not and never can be mine.

He spoke, of course, from experience. Married three times, he had had three angels in his house, but from this almost excessive wealth of material was able to produce only triteness and commonplace.

As a violent corrective to smugness and banality comes at this point the pagan singing of Swinburne. Pagan, primitive and lusty—anti-Victorian :

> Love, that is first and last of all things made,
> The light that has the living world for shade . . .
> Love, that is flesh upon the spirit of man
> And spirit within the flesh whence breath began ;
> Love, that keeps all the choir of lives in chime ;
> Love, that is blood within the veins of time . . .
> That binds on all men's feet or chains or wings ;
> Love, that is root and fruit of terrene things—

—and so on, impetuously, tumultuously, for many lines. Salutary as was his attitude at this time, unfortunately his poems perpetually lose themselves in a superabundance of words : like so many rivers running inevitably into marshland. They have no beginning and no end : they are all middle. And though glorious, quick and blood-stirring his rhythms and rimes—

> We have heard from hidden places
>   What love scarce lives and hears :
> We have seen on fervent faces
>   The pallor of strange tears :

C

> We have trod the wine-vat's treasure,
>   Whence, ripe to steam and stain,
>   Foams round the feet of pleasure
>   The blood-red must of pain ;

again, as with the Elizabethans, our heart is not touched, only our senses are pleasantly stung. Swinburne's love is mere academic love—copied after old models— literary love : a playing with words. The figure jerks its arms and legs, its head moves—but it is only a puppet of sawdust after all. We watch for a while, our interest caught, then the jiggings quickly become monotonous and tire us at last.

But Swinburne served a good purpose, nevertheless. It was impossible in the wild gust of his song for the smug and the trite to flourish : to him must go the credit for delivering love from the prison of domestication.

§

ON LIFE

Since I am dealing separately in other chapters with the poetry of religion (the mystical approach to the Deity)—equally with love the leading preoccupation of mankind—and the several chief kinds of lyric verse ; there remains to be approached here the considerable body of what may be termed Reflective Lyrics : meditations in general. The business of living is not only a business, but an art as well ; and it is proper that art should consider it, analyze it, and comment upon it in all its aspects. On the whole, the poets are fervidly agreed that, as a business, it is bad, and as an art, it is difficult. Of course, one need not be a poet to concur with such obvious findings. But there is more in it—more " to it," as the saying goes—than that ; and it is from the poets that we learn in what that more consists : the subtleties, the refinements, the infinite gradations that emphasize, or alleviate, the fundamental badness and difficulty.

In the battle between the optimists and the pessimists, it is the pessimists that seem at a first glance to have it all their own way. The champions of optimism are few. We think at once of three or four names—and the rest is silence. Or, rather, pessimism.

There is Browning with his bluff shout :

> The year's at the Spring,
> And day's at the morn ;
> Morning's at seven ;
> The hill-side's dew-pearled ;
> The lark's on the wing ;
> The snail's on the thorn ;
> God's in his heaven—
> All's right with the world !

—but it is, we feel, the easy, unconvincing and unthinking heartiness of a healthy man fresh from his cold tub and expectant of a substantial breakfast. We cannot refrain from picturing the reverse of the medal : supposing the year was at winter ; a dense fog wrapped the scene ; the hill-side was sodden with mud and fallen leaves ; the lark was sensibly fled to a more suitable climate for winging and singing in ; and the past night had been one of insomnia—how then ? The conclusion of God's being in his heaven and all being right with the world would not, perhaps, come so pat to the mind.

There is Whitman, with his ebullient belief in everything, good and evil ; but we feel with him that the elementary virtue of discrimination is sadly needed—

and sadly lacking. What can one do with
a man who cancels himself out so deftly
and completely with the defiant remark :
" Do I contradict myself ? Very well,
then, I contradict myself " ?

Who, then, is left ? There is the plain-
tive Clough :

> Say not the struggle nought availeth ;

and Tennyson—shall we say ? :

> I hope to see my Pilot face to face,
> When I have crossed the bar.

But no ; the " hope " is too faint, too
timid to enrol Tennyson among the optimists. Neither he nor Clough is sufficiently
positive. There remains Milton, splendidly
sure—declaring

> . . . Eternity shall greet our bliss
> With an individual kiss ;
> And Joy shall overtake us as a flood . . .
> Attir'd with Stars, we shall for ever sit,
> Triumphing over Death, and Chance, and thee O
> Time.

—Magnificent lines, matching a magnificent faith.

But if the optimists are few in the lists,
we discover the thorough-paced pessimists
to be no more numerous. Delicately poised

between the two extremes stands the majority of the poets ; preserving a stoical attitude ; with little hope and less fear. The Elizabethan, John Davies, speaks for them all in brave simplicity :

> I know myself a Man—
> Which is a proud and wretched thing.

And that acceptance is echoed in Housman :

> The troubles of our proud and angry dust
> Are from eternity, and shall not fail ;
> Bear them we can, and if we can we must.

There are no compensations to be looked for in acquiescence of our fate ;—though we be angry we are also proud. We must realize that the glory of being a man is a sterile glory. To question is instinctive enough, but—we are warned :

> Since Knowledge is but Sorrow's spy,
> It is not safe to know.

There ensues, then, that bitter, or gentle, summing-up of the totality of things by the thwarted spirit in the stark words of the Preacher : " Vanity of vanities ; All is vanity."

We are creatures of change and chance ; lapped in incessant ebb and flow ; the one thing constant in the eternal flux is the undeparting vanity informing all, and the certainty that, soon or late,

> The glory of the sum of things
> Will flash along the chords and go.

Would we, Webster asks, " seek by trophies and dead things To leave a living name behind ? " If so, we merely " weave but nets to catch the wind."

Shirley puts it explicitly :

> The glories of our blood and state
> Are shadows, not substantial things ;
> There is no armour against Fate ;
> Death lays his icy hand on kings ;
> Sceptre and crown
> Must tumble down,
> And in the dust be equal made
> With the poor crooked scythe and spade.

—a sombre statement that echoes Shakespeare's

> Golden lads and girls all must,
> As chimney-sweepers, come to dust ;

and Housman's most melodious :

> The lofty shade advances,
> I fetch my flute and play :
> Come, lads, and learn the dances
> And praise the tune to-day.
> To-morrow, more's the pity,
> Away we both must hie,
> To air the ditty,
> And to earth I.

But the inevitable may be faced with a smile ; and if life be short and dissolution certain, still there are pleasures to be enjoyed along the way :

> Let us drink and be merry, dance, joke and rejoice,
> With claret and sherry, theorbo and voice !
> The changeable world to our joy is unjust,
>   All treasure's uncertain,
>   Then down with your dust !
> In frolics dispose your pounds, shillings and pence,
> For we shall be nothing a hundred years hence.

The wiser mind, however, will be moderate, remembering always that a surfeit produces nausea ; that life is essentially an art whose intricate and delicate exercise is at once marred by the violent crudity of excess.

The one inescapable thing, all the while, is the pathetic brevity of life. All art, it may be said, is a brave attempt to arrest the transient ; to keep bright and luscious for ever the flowers and fruits of insight while all else withers around them. Art is man's inadequate gesture in the face of inexorable decay.

The gentle Herrick, contemplating daffodils, laments :

We have short time to stay, as you,
   We have as short a spring ;
As quick a growth to meet decay,
   As you, or anything.
     We die
   As your hours do, and dry
     Away
Like to the summer's rain ;
Or as the pearls of morning's dew,
   Ne'er to be found again.

In the dust and heat of the day, in the still hours of the night, there is no pause for mortality on its " long fool's errand to the grave " :

But at my back I always hear
Time's winged chariot hurrying near,
And yonder all before me lie
Deserts of vast eternity.

The harassed mind yearns for escape and refuge. " I long," cries Clare—" I long for scenes where man has never trod." Truly, " The world is too much with us." Keats, listening to the nightingale, aches to

Fade far away, dissolve, and quite forget . . .
The weariness, the fever and the fret
  Here, where men sit and hear each other groan ;
Where palsy shakes a few, sad, last grey hairs,
  Where youth grows pale, and spectre-thin, and
    dies ;

Where but to think is to be full of sorrow
   And leaden-eyed despairs ;
Where beauty cannot keep her lustrous eyes,
   Or new Love pine at them beyond to-morrow.

But the surest refuge is ever in man himself : he carries with him wherever he
goes the dreaming meadows, the still lakes
of his imagination. Useless to wander
farther ; there is no refuge in life surer :
the quest is vain. Even so, it is not
enough ; we can only pause,

And wish the long unhappy dream would end,
   And waive all claim to bliss, and try to bear
With close-lipp'd patience for our only friend,
   Sad patience, too near neighbour to despair.

This is the conclusion of the whole
matter. At the last, " sad patience,"
whose other name is resignation, guides
our feet, not unwilling, to the final refuge
of the grave.

CHAPTER IV

GIVE SORROW WORDS

§

THE great soul of the poet reaches one of its noblest heights in the Elegy. Here, faced with the profound mystery of death, it contemplates the equally profound mysteries of birth and life, of chance and fate. It mourns and seeks consolation; armed with the weapons of suffering and dismay, it demands from enduring silence the all-sufficing Answer; and the measure of its passionate audacity is the measure of its loftiest nobility.

THE MAJOR ELEGIES

In "Lycidas," Milton laments the death by drowning of a college friend in language whose grandeur is unapproached in the range of our literature. But the poem, cast in classical pastoral form, expresses no obvious sincerity of grief, no intimate sense of loss. Beginning with conventional expressions of sorrow, the poet reserves the full strength of his feeling for a denunciation of the clergy of the time. But the actual subject-matter of the piece is, for once, of little importance. What is important is the majestic march of the ordered lines : laden with breath-taking loveliness. Sumptuous imagery abounds, and the whole is informed with a music whose melting sweetness overcomes the ear. Listen :

> He must not float upon his watery bier
> Unwept, and welter to the parching wind,
> Without the meed of some melodious tear.

The alliteration is magical ; the effect sensuous in the extreme. Here, a daring image of the dawning :

> Together both, ere the high lawns appeared
> Under the opening eye-lids of the morn,
> We drove afield. . . .

—daring indeed, but the daring of a master. This passage of rich delights :

Return, Sicilian Muse,
And call the vales, and bid them hither cast
Their bells, and flow'rets of a thousand hues.
Ye valleys low. . . .
Throw hither all your quaint enamelled eyes,
That on the green turf suck the honied showers,
And purple all the ground with vernal flowers . . .
Bid Amaranthus all his beauty shed,
And daffadillies fill their cups with tears,
To strew the laureate hearse where Lycid lies.

And this, of tenderest felicity :

Weep no more, woful Shepherds, weep no more,
For Lycidas your sorrow is not dead,
Sunk though he be beneath the watery floor. . . .
With nectar pure his oozy locks he laves,
And hears the unexpressive nuptial song,
In the blest kingdoms meek of joy and love.
There entertain him all the Saints above,
In solemn troops, and sweet societies
That sing, and singing in their glory move,
And wipe the tears forever from his eyes.

With Gray's " Elegy Written in a
Country Churchyard " the soaring note is
lost, the sensuous music vanished. We are
in the eighteenth century with Pope,
Johnson and Goldsmith, and poetry has
taken on some of the attributes of rhetoric.

There was a man once (so legends tells)
who, after witnessing " Hamlet " for the
first time, and asked what he thought of it,

replied : " Oh, not much. It was just full of quotations." That man would undoubtedly have made the same remark after a first reading of Gray's " Elegy." For, more than any other poem in the language, it has enjoyed a constant and vast popularity, and this no doubt by reason not only of its illustration throughout of everyday and obvious reflections, but also of their aphoristic presentation. The following lines have passed long since into the currency of our speech :

> The short and simple annals of the poor.

> The paths of glory lead but to the grave.

> Far from the madding crowd's ignoble strife.

And so have these phrases : " The boast of heraldry," " the pomp of power," " storied urn," " chill Penury," " some mute inglorious Milton," " one longing ling'ring look." And is there any other stanza in English poetry better known than this ?—

> Full many a gem of purest ray serene,
> The dark unfathom'd caves of ocean bear :
> Full many a flower is born to blush unseen,
> And waste its sweetness on the desert air.

We had need of these sentiments to be put so pithily, so precisely, so gracefully, commonplace as they are. They receive in the " Elegy " a habitation for all time.

The return from rhetoric is splendidly accomplished in Shelley's " Adonaïs," where the poet commemorates the untimely death of his fellow-poet, John Keats. The high note is recaptured once more ; imagery and melody reappear in rapt partnership. The poem progresses through lovely and moving lamentation to an eloquent and triumphant conclusion.

> I weep for Adonaïs—he is dead !

Adonaïs—Keats. Just as Adonaïs was dear to Aphrodite, so was Keats to Urania, goddess of Heavenly Love and Muse of high poetry.

> Ah, woe is me ! Winter is come and gone,
> But grief returns with the revolving year—

It is the experience of all who have lived and suffered loss :

> Alas ! that all we loved of him should be,
> But for our grief, as if it had not been,
> And grief itself be mortal !

But soon the heart is lifted ; a sudden thought has woken and grown into certainty :

> Peace, peace ! he is not dead, he doth not sleep—
> He hath awakened from the dream of life—

the poet's vision sees, astoundingly, Death and Life change places :

> He lives, he wakes—'tis Death is dead, not he ;

while we, the living :

> > We decay
> > Like corpses in a charnel.

We must no longer mourn for Adonaïs, for, lo :

> He has outsoared the shadow of our night ;
> Envy and calumny and hate and pain,
> And that unrest which men miscall delight,
> Can touch him not and torture not again ;
> From the contagion of the world's slow stain
> He is secure——

He has attained to uttermost bliss :

> > He is made one with Nature . . .
> > He is a portion of the loveliness
> > Which once he made more lovely . . .

Uttermost bliss, since :

> The One remains, the many change and pass ;
> Heaven's light forever shines, Earth's shadows fly ;
> Life, like a dome of many-coloured glass,
> Stains the white radiance of eternity,
> Until Death tramples it to fragments. . . .

The close of the poem is sonorous with organ-like music of majesty and triumphant finality.

Tennyson's " In Memoriam " is the longest as well as the most personal of the great elegies. It gives expression not only to the poet's poignant grief at the early death of his friend, Arthur Hallam, but also to the whole conflict of a mind clinging to a religious and ideal conception of life with the naturalistic trend of thought of the time. The developments of biological science and historical criticism were altering the entire character of the clash between faith and reason, and Tennyson seeks in " In Memoriam " to make the idea of evolution a reconciliation. The argument in all its ramifications is too complex to be detailed here. A brief outline will suffice to show the poem's movement along the

D

paths of suffering and doubt toward the sanctuary of hope and faith.

The grief at first is intense, overwhelming ; the poet is " widowed " ; the beloved friend is to him

> Dear as the mother to the son,
> More than my brothers are to me.

Then Memory slowly brings back the happy days past, spent together, and the confession is wrung from him after some hesitation that

> 'Tis better to have loved and lost
> Than never to have loved at all.

Nevertheless, bereavement has changed his world :

> With weary steps I loiter on,
>   Though always under altered skies
>   The purple from the distance dies,
> My prospect and horizon gone.

He wonders : How fares it with the happy dead ? but no answer comes to quiet his doubts, to sustain his flagging faith. He questions the inscrutable workings of the universe, as others before him, and in the following pause reaches the helpless conviction :

Behold, we know not anything ;
  I can but trust that good shall fall
  At last—far off—at last, to all,
And every winter change to spring.

It is the last hope of one round whom
has gathered the darkness of intellectual
despair :

       But what am I ?
        An infant crying in the night :
        An infant crying for the light :
       And with no language but a cry.

And in the unassuageable darkness :

    I falter where I firmly trod,
    And falling with my weight of cares
      Upon the great world's altar-stairs
    That slope thro' darkness up to God,

    I stretch lame hands of faith, and grope,
      And gather dust and chaff, and call
      To what I feel is Lord of all,
    And faintly trust the larger hope.

But the " faint hope " persists—it is the
sole gleam in the settled darkness :

    For tho' my lips may breathe adieu,
    I cannot think the thing farewell.

He seizes on it desperately, and tends it
to a glow. Gradually the glow becomes a
radiance : the spiritual conviction that,
despite all seeming evidence to the contrary,

Death does not conquer Love, does not conquer Life Eternal :

> Dear friend, far off, my lost desire,
>   So far, so near in woe and weal ;
>   O loved the most, when most I feel
> There is a lower and a higher ;
>
> Known and unknown ; human, divine ;
>   Sweet human hand and lips and eye ;
>   Dear heavenly friend that canst not die,
> Mine, mine, for ever, ever mine :

and the poem draws to a conclusion on a note of solemn, but exultant, affirmation :

> Thy voice is on the rolling air ;
>   I hear thee where the waters run ;
>   Thou standest in the rising sun,
> And in the setting thou art fair.
>
> What art thou then ?   I cannot guess ;
>   But tho' I seem in star and flower
>   To feel thee some diffusive power,
> I do not therefore love thee less :
>
> My love involves the love before ;
>   My love is vaster passion now ;
>   Tho' mixed with God and Nature thou,
> I seem to love thee more and more.
>
> Far off thou art, but ever nigh ;
>   I love thee still, and I rejoice ;
>   I prosper, circled with thy voice ;
> I shall not lose thee tho' I die.

In Matthew Arnold's "Thyrsis"—a lament for the poet Arthur Hugh Clough— the note is far less impassioned, far less personal, than that of "In Memoriam." The poet looks on life as a doubtful gift, to be accepted in a spirit of stoic acquiescence rather than with eagerness and delight. It is not to religion that he turns for consolation in the time of his loss, but to nature and art : the English landscape and classical literature. The poem is a pastoral elegy, loaded with fine descriptions of the country-side around Oxford, "that sweet city with her dreaming spires." The poet wanders through the well-remembered fields where he was so often wont to walk with Thyrsis in the past :

> I know these slopes ; who knows them if not I ?—
> But many a dingle on the loved hill-side,
>   With thorns once studded, old white-blossom'd
>   trees,
>   Where thick the cowslips grew, and, far descried,
>   High tower'd the spikes of purple orchises,
>   Hath since our day put by
>   The coronals of that forgotten time ;
>   Down each green bank hath gone the plough-
>   boy's team,
>   And only in the hidden brookside gleam
> Primroses, orphans of the flowery prime.

> Where is the girl, who by the boatman's door,
>   Above the locks, above the boating throng,
>   Unmoor'd our skiff, when, through the Wytham
>   flats,
>   Red loosestrife and blond meadowsweet among,
>   And darting swallows, and light water-gnats,
>   We track'd the shy Thames shore ?
>   Where are the mowers, who, as the tiny swell
>   Of our boat passing heaved the river-grass,
>   Stood with suspended scythe to see us pass ?
>   They all are gone, and thou art gone as well.

Before he died, Thyrsis' piping had taken on " a troubled sound," had

> learnt a stormy note,
> Of men contention-tost, of men who groan—

he sang, and lived, unhappily ; but now he is at peace. The poet, himself unhappy and contention-tost, can but follow in his steps. And when fatigue and fear assail, he will recall that Thyrsis went steadfastly on, until he fell : " I wandered till I died "; and strengthened by his example he, too, will somehow pace out the sorry walk of life.

The poem, for all its austerity of argument, its rather chill philosophy, is verbally richly wrought. Only in one other piece—

" The Scholar Gipsy "—does Arnold write so faithfully and lovingly, so completely satisfyingly, of the English country-side.

THE MINOR ELEGIES

So much, then, for the large canvases in Sorrow's gallery ; now for the Miniatures Room.

Here, in briefest compass, with a minimum of strokes, as it were, we find expressed all the essentials of the larger pieces. If those may be said to be abiding-places of the spirit, these are guesting-houses by the way.

The poignancy of untimely death, of youth being cut down in its flower, is tenderly and movingly recorded in Hartley Coleridge's " Early Death," a lyric that has much of Wordsworth's unstrained simplicity in it :

> She passed away like morning dew
>   Before the sun was high ;
> So brief her time, she scarcely knew
>   The meaning of a sigh.

As round the rose its soft perfume,
  Sweet love around her floated ;
Admired she grew—while mortal doom
  Crept on, unfear'd, unnoted.

Love was her guardian Angel here,
  But Love to Death resign'd her ;
Tho' Love was kind, why should we fear
  But holy Death is kinder ?

Wilde's " Requiescat," with the same subject, is slighter, but no less moving :

Tread lightly, she is near
  Under the snow,
Speak gently, she can hear
  The daisies grow. . . .

Lily-like, white as snow,
  She hardly knew
She was a woman, so
  Sweetly she grew.

Coffin-board, heavy stone,
  Lie on her breast,
I vex my heart alone,
  She is at rest. . . .

Browning's wistful " Beautiful Evelyn Hope is dead " has resignation for the present and hope for the future—hope for

an eventual meeting in the hereafter. That
intensely-desired hereafter haunts Poe:

> And all my days are trances,
>   And all my nightly dreams
> Are where thy grey eye glances,
>   And where thy footstep gleams—
> In what ethereal dances,
>   By what eternal streams.

But Tennyson cries out in his dire loneliness for comfort here and now:

> Oh that 'twere possible
> After long grief and pain
> To find the arms of my true love
> Round me once again! . . .

> A shadow flits before me,
> Not thou, but like to thee:
> Ah Christ, that it were possible
> For one short hour to see
> The souls we loved, that they might tell us
> What and where they be. . . .

> Half the night I waste in sighs,
> Half in dreams I follow after
> The delight of early skies;
> In a wakeful doze I sorrow
> For the hand, the lips, the eyes,
> For the meeting of the morrow,
> The delight of happy laughter,
> The delight of low replies.

He reiterates the cry in another poem, one of the supreme lyrics in the language, where the "Break, break" of the sea becomes the breaking of a human heart :

> Break, break, break,
>   On thy cold grey stones, O Sea !
> And I would that my tongue could utter
>   The thoughts that arise in me.
>
> O well for the fisherman's boy
>   That he shouts with his sister at play !
> O well for the sailor lad
>   That he sings in his boat on the bay !
>
> And the stately ships go on
>   To their haven under the hill ;
> But O for the touch of a vanish'd hand,
>   And the sound of a voice that is still !
>
> Break, break, break,
>   At the foot of thy crags, O Sea !
> But the tender grace of a day that is dead
>   Will never come back to me.

The realization of Nevermore is the bitterest of all human experiences to face and accept. With the loss of the beloved all the ways of earth become barren and profitless. Life has nothing, henceforth, to hold, save only the

now-desired, deep-coveted gift of Death.
Alexander Smith gives pathetic voice to
this in " Barbara " :

> In vain, in vain, in vain !
>   You will never come again.
> There drops upon the dreary hills a mournful
>   fringe of rain ;
> The gloaming closes slowly round, loud winds are
>   in the tree ;
> Round selfish shores forever moans the hurt and
>   wounded sea ;
> There is no rest upon the earth, peace is with Death
>   and thee,
>   Barbara !

" No rest upon the earth "—Matthew
Arnold's gentle " Requiescat " is of a
woman, presumably an actress, who, tired
of the world and its people, longed for
solitude and peace, and at length attained
them in death.   We are not to mourn : she
has her desire :

> Strew on her roses, roses,
>   And never a spray of yew.
> In quiet she reposes :
>   Ah ! would that I did too.
>
> Her mirth the world required :
>   She bathed it in smiles of glee.
> But her heart was tired, tired,
>   And now they let her be.

Her life was turning, turning,
  In mazes of heat and sound.
But for peace her soul was yearning,
  And now peace laps her round.

Her cabin'd, ample Spirit,
  It flutter'd and fail'd for breath.
To-night it doth inherit
  The vasty hall of Death.

Lovely as that is : simple, direct and
poignant : when set beside Landor's " Rose
Aylmer " it appears overlong, diffuse in
statement, mechanical almost in melody.
The eight lines of " Rose Aylmer " comprise another of the most magical lyrics
in the language : restrained, concentrated,
of the utmost pathos, the first three lines
a series of general statement, the remaining
five a particular application of the series.
The lines, musically, are a chain of sighs :

Ah, what avails the sceptred race !
  Ah, what the form divine !
What every beauty, every grace !
  Rose Aylmer, all were thine.

Rose Aylmer, whom these wakeful eyes
  May weep, but never see,
A night of memories and sighs
  I consecrate to thee.

Such, then, the Elegy.   It will be seen that, borne irresistibly upward on the wings of his sorrow, the poet achieves one of the noblest heights compassable by the human spirit.

CHAPTER V

SERMONS IN STONES

§

THE Englishman's love of his country is not simply and solely a patriotic love of an abstraction. It is, at core, a deeply personal and intimate love for the " green and pleasant land " in which he lives :

This royal throne of kings, this sceptr'd isle,
This earth of majesty, this seat of Mars,
This other Eden, demi-paradise,
This fortress built by Nature for herself
Against infection and the hand of war . . .
This precious stone set in the silver sea . . .
This blessed plot, this earth, this realm, this
    England.

The poets express this love faithfully and ardently in a constant and careful picturing of the familiar abounding villages, hills, fields, and streams. No other country's poetry is so rich as England's in delineations and interpretations of Nature.

Just as in the sister art of painting, landscape was introduced at first only as a minor contribution to the picture, so Nature was at first introduced into poetry —only as asides unimportant and insignificant : mere decoration. The first picture to be painted consisting entirely of landscape was an astonishing innovation, but once the way was shewn other painters were not slow to take it. And so was it in poetry. From the brief mentions in the early poets to the almost complete preoccupation of Wordsworth and succeeding poets is an impressive development.

It is not too much to say that the path to an understanding of the English character lies in the study of English Nature poetry.

§

But it is with English poetry as with all other countries' poetry : man, questing for the key to his own mysterious soul and the bewildering universe about him, turns instinctively to Nature. Surely—he feels—if he pierce deeply enough down, he will come upon it laid close to the great pervading heart. He delves deliberately, but if the key seems, with all his labour, still as remote as ever, other and glittering treasures are, almost compensatingly, un-covered as he toils :

> One impulse from a vernal wood
>   May teach you more of man,
> Of moral evil and of good,
>   Than all the sages can.
>
> Sweet is the love that Nature brings ;
>   Our meddling intellect
> Misshapes the beauteous forms of things :
>   —We murder to dissect.
>
> Enough of science and of art ;
>   Close up these barren leaves :
> Come forth, and bring with you a heart
>   That watches and receives.

Wordsworth, more than any other poet, " watched " Nature, and " received " from her ; and of him it may well be said what he wrote of " The Poet " :

> The outward shows of sky and earth,
> Of hill and valley, he has view'd ;
> And impulses of deeper birth
> Have come to him in solitude.

In common things that round us lie
Some random truths he can impart,
—The harvest of a quiet eye
That broods and sleeps on his own heart.

Wordsworth is constantly linking up recollections of his childhood with his meditations upon Nature. The two become complementary : halves that, brought together, constitute a perfect whole—his vision of ultimate truth. We trace it throughout his work. Listening to the cuckoo :

O blessèd bird ! the earth we pace
Again appears to be
An unsubstantial, faëry place
That is fit home for thee !

—Observing a rainbow :

My heart leaps up when I behold
A rainbow in the sky :
So was it when my life began ;
So is it now I am a man . . .

—On a nutting expedition, when, having despoiled the hazels and about to leave the bower, he feels a "sense of pain " on looking at the " silent trees and the intruding sky," and senses with a sudden reverent excitement that " there is a spirit in the woods."

Always there is this expression of high wonder, that springs alike from the white innocence of remembered childhood and the untainted innocence of the child-in-the-man. It reaches its most perfect expression in the ode, " Intimations of Immortality from Recollections of Early Childhood," which is too long to give here, and must be read attentively in its entirety.

It is in the " Lines Composed near Tintern Abbey " that Wordsworth, the teacher, mystic and seer, voices his *Credo* nobly and enduringly:

> I have learned (he says),
> To look on Nature, not as in the hour
> Of thoughtless youth ; but hearing oftentimes
> The still, sad music of humanity . . .
>   And I have felt
> A presence that disturbs me with the joy
> Of elevated thoughts ; a sense sublime
> Of something far more deeply interfused,
> Whose dwelling is the light of setting suns,
> And the round ocean and the living air,
> And the blue sky, and in the mind of man :
> A motion and a spirit, that impels
> All thinking things, all objects of all thought,
> And rolls through all things.   Therefore am I still
> A lover of the meadows and the woods,
> And mountains ; and of all that we behold
> From this green earth ; of all the mighty world

Of eye, and ear—both what they half create,
And what perceive ; well pleased to recognize
In nature and the language of the sense,
The anchor of my purest thoughts, the nurse,
The guide, the guardian of my heart, and soul
Of all my moral being.

These majestic lines, that are the very
stuff of humanity at its most sublime,
contain the *core* of Wordsworth's life-long
thought and his considered message.

§

But such Nature poetry represents the
peaks of achievement. There are the plains
—unurgent, gracious, easier of tread—also.
Here we come on no moralizing, but a
picturing of the seasons and their changeful
contents, for the sheer delight in doing
so. No stress of search and questioning,
but a calm and restful acceptance : refresh-
ment and recreation for the spirit.

How soothingly Collins begins his " Ode
to Evening " :

If aught of oaten stop, or pastoral song,
May hope, chaste Eve, to soothe thy modest ear,
    Like thy own solemn springs,
    Thy springs and dying gales ;

and the poem continues serenely to its serene conclusion :

> So long, regardful of thy quiet rule,
> Shall Fancy, Friendship, Science, rose-lipp'd Health
>   Thy gentlest influence own,
>   And hymn thy favourite name !

the cadences, so evenly unostentatious, so perfectly modulated, seem scarcely to break the silence, but sing rather to the listening inner ear of the soul.

Blake's fresh and musical apostrophe " To Spring " :

> O thou with dewy locks, who lookest down
> Through the clear windows of the morning, turn
> Thine angel eyes upon our western isle,
> Which in full choir hails thy approach, O
>   Spring ! . . .

> Come o'er the eastern hills, and let our winds
> Kiss thy perfumed garments ; let us taste
> Thy morn and evening breath ; scatter thy pearls
> Upon our lovesick land that mourns for thee—

(which recalls Collins, but is imbued with a freedom and enthusiasm Collins never knew) brings to mind Shelley's delicious " To Night " :

Swiftly walk over the western wave,
      Spirit of Night !
Out of the misty eastern cave
Where, all the long and lone daylight,
Thou wovest dreams of joy and fear
Which make thee terrible and dear,
      Swift be thy flight !

Wrap thy form in a mantle grey,
      Star-inwrought,
Blind with thine hair the eyes of Day ;
Kiss her until she be wearied out.
Then wander o'er city and sea and land,
Touching all with thine opiate wand—
      Come, long-sought !

With Keats—foreshadowing the later Tennyson—we reach a fullness of orchestration never before attempted. The " Ode to Autumn " emphasizes the splendour and profuse fruition of the season ; its note is sounded in the first line : " Season of mists and mellow fruitfulness " ; it ignores the encroaching decay and the year's declension. The last stanza is superbly pictorial :

Where are the songs of Spring ? Ay, where are
    they ?
Think not of them, thou hast thy music too,—
While barred clouds bloom the soft-dying day,
And touch the stubble-plains with rosy hue ;
Then in a wailful choir the small gnats mourn

Among the river sallows, borne aloft
Or sinking as the light wind lives or dies ;
And full-grown lambs loud bleat from hilly bourn ;
Hedge-crickets sing ; and now with treble soft
The redbreast whistles from a garden-croft ;
And gathering swallows twitter in the skies.

But it is when we come to Tennyson that we find Nature delineated with superlative felicity and aptness : a meticulous observation wedded to precise language. No poet has a more loving eye for the small details of the physical world, as may be seen from the following several examples selected at random from the many scattered throughout his work :

To-day I saw the dragon-fly
Come from the wells where he did lie.

An inner impulse rent the veil
Of his old husk : from head to tail
Came out clear plates of sapphire mail.

He dried his wings : like gauze they grew :
Through crofts and pastures wet with dew
A living flash of light he flew.

*   *   *

Laburnums, dropping-wells of fire.

*   *   *

When rosy plumelets tuft the larch.

*   *   *

The sunflower, shining fair,
Ray(s) round with flames her disk of seed.

*   *   *

Ice
Makes daggers at the sharpen'd eaves.

*   *   *

The monstrous ledges . . . spill
Their thousand wreaths of dangling water-smoke.

*   *   *

The wrinkled sea.

*   *   *

A million emeralds break from the ruby-budded
    lime.

*   *   *

The dry-tongued laurels' pattering talk.

Tennyson, in his descriptive vein, was
invariably pictorial. With fewest and
simplest words he could conjure up a
scene and stretch it before the mind's eye
unforgettably. Think of "The Lotos-
Eaters," for instance—to read which is like

viewing a lofty chamber hung with a series of glowing tapestries woven with gorgeous thread. Think of the opening lines of " Œnone " ; of " The Lady of Shalott " (as prophetic of William Morris as Keats of Tennyson) ; of " Mariana " ; portions of " Maud " and " In Memoriam " ; and " The Dying Swan." This last in particular is an excellent example of his graphic portrayal :

> The plain was grassy, wild and bare,
> Wide, wild, and open to the air,
> Which had built up everywhere
>   An under-roof of doleful grey.
> With an inner voice the river ran,
> Adown it floated a dying swan,
>   And loudly did lament.
>   It was the middle of the day.
> Ever the weary wind went on,
>   And took the reed-tops as it went.

And this—" Tithonus "—contains in its opening four lines a magnificent compression : all autumn and all of autumn's melancholy :

> The woods decay, the woods decay and fall,
> The vapours weep their burthen to the ground ;
> Man comes and tills the field and lies beneath,
> And after many a summer dies the swan.

Browning, properly speaking, was no Nature poet : people, with their minds and their actions, were his chief interest. Matthew Arnold, likewise—apart from " Thyrsis " and " The Scholar Gipsy," which contain many beautiful descriptive passages—wrote little of Nature, but much of spiritual and intellectual problems. William Morris did no more than use it superficially as a decoration ; and one feels the same with Rossetti and Swinburne.

Wordsworth and Tennyson, then, stand out from all their fellows as the supreme Nature poets ; the one interpretative, the other delineative. The one that concerned himself, so to speak, with Nature's elusive soul ; the other, with her alluring body.

CHAPTER VI

SCANTY PLOT OF GROUND

§

THE Sonnet, by its fixed length of fourteen lines and its prescribed and complex riming scheme, is a rigid and difficult form. Though most poets have used it, only a few—Shakespeare, Milton, Wordsworth, Keats and Rossetti—have found in its constriction "not bonds but wings," others—Coleridge, Shelley and Arnold—felt definitely cramped by it; Byron and Tennyson never practised it, and Browning despised it.

But if the Sonnet is one of the lesser jewels in our poetry's crown, it is nevertheless not lacking in brilliancy.

Except on rare occasions (to two of which I shall come later), it is not employed when passion is at white heat—for obvious reasons : the involved strictures of form are so many obstacles in the way of spontaneous composition. Rather is it resorted to in moods of rumination and meditation, when the tide of passion is subdued somewhat. Another use is as an embodiment of didactics, in which it has come—since the Romantic Revival—to take the place of the tending-to-be-epigrammatic sets of heroic couplets.

Though it need not have the " singing " quality of a lyric, it is essential that most careful attention be paid by the poet to the vowel-construction of the lines, that the sibilants be disciplined, and that full use be made of the device of subtle and concealed alliterations. Hence, the poet's rhythmic impulse needs to be stimulated, not crippled, by the use of rime and the satisfaction of technical demands. By its briefness and close-knittedness, it will be seen that the Sonnet is the ideal vehicle for the economic expression and rounded working-out of a single thought.

Though the Elizabethans had something of a fashion for writing linked series of sonnets, and though one or two later

poets, Elizabeth Barrett Browning and
Dante Gabriel Rossetti, each wrote a
similar series, the practice—hardly more
than a literary *tour de force*—has fallen
since into desuetude. Not regrettably—
Shakespeare's hundred and fifty-four apart
—the sonnet by its very nature is fitted,
and is able, to stand alone.

In his two sonnets on the Sonnet, Wordsworth states the case for use of the form
admirably. He says : the Sonnet is not
to be scorned, nor tribute to be withheld
from it, by the critic, when the use is
remembered to which it was put by Shakespeare, Petrarch, Tasso, Camœns, Dante,
Spenser and Milton. For himself, as
" Nuns fret not at their convent's narrow
room, And hermits are contented with
their cells," he is content, on occasion,
when distracted by " the weight of too
much liberty " (i.e., verse-forms of greater
freedom), to be bound " within the Sonnet's
scanty plot of ground," and to find there
" brief solace."

§

The "problems" of Shakespeare's
sonnet-series have long perplexed scholar-
ship. They are many and intricate : the
curious enigma of the dedication ; the
identity of the chief characters—the " man
right fair " ; the rival poet ; the " woman
colour'd ill " ;—and even whether the series
be allegorical, or strictly personal, or partly
personal and partly dramatic. But these
conundrums need not be inquired into
here ; they are of pedantic interest only.
Sufficient is it to accept the sonnets as they
stand—a series remarkable no less for
their " story " than for their innumerable
beauties. The general theme is the poet's
almost idolatrous love for a younger friend,
a noble youth (his " better angel "); and
his only less passionate, but more troubled,
love for a woman (" the worser spirit ").
The woman, after a similar attempt by the
rival writer, wins the youth away from the
poet, who, after passing through doubt,
distrust, jealousy and estrangement, even-
tually forgives him whole-heartedly and

loves him as devotedly as before. In these hundred and fifty-four sonnets, the whole spiritual territory of love is ranged over and meticulously mapped.

It is not easy, nor desirable, to select for quotation here any one of the sonnets; they are a string of perfectly matched gems, and were better admired in their continuity. The lustre of each is enhanced by the lustre imparted by its neighbours. The collection is unique in our poetry, and the careful study of it will yield inexhaustible profit to the reader.

Previous to Shakespeare, we have other sonnet-productions of merit, though not of superlative merit. Sir Philip Sidney's

Leave me, O Love, which reachest but to dust,
And thou, my mind, aspire to higher things !

is melodious and tender; as is Samuel Daniel's

Fair is my Love, and cruel as she's fair ;

and Fletcher's " Licia," Constable's " Diana " and Spenser's " Amoretti." But this sonnet melodiousness-and-tenderness seems but the prevailing lyric of the time dressed in different form. Even the finest of them all—Drayton's

> Since there's no help, come let us kiss and part—

lovely and moving as it is, one feels could have been written in typical lyrical fashion without loss ; it does not urgently *demand* the sonnet form, instantly rejecting all others, as one instinctively feels to be the case with Milton, writing in a gust of passionate wrath, " On the Late Massacre in Piemont " :

> Avenge, O Lord, Thy slaughter'd Saints, whose bones
> Lie scatter'd on the Alpine mountains cold,
> Ev'n them who kept Thy truth so pure of old
> When all our Fathers worshipp'd Stocks and Stones,
> Forget not : in Thy book record their groans
> Who were Thy Sheep and in their ancient Fold
> Slain by the bloody Piemontese that roll'd
> Mother and Infant down the Rocks. Their moans
> The Vales redoubl'd to the Hills, and they
> To Heav'n. Their martyr'd blood and ashes sow
> O'er all th' Italian fields where still doth sway
> The triple Tyrant : that from these may grow
> A hundred-fold, who having learnt Thy way,
> Early may fly the Babylonian woe.

This magnificent denunciation, sonorous, terrific, is perfectly and inevitably contained in its fourteen lines, and one cannot imagine its expression in any other metrical form.

But Milton was a supreme master of the sonnet.   How perfect and inevitable, again, the one on his blindness :

> When I consider how my light is spent,
> Ere half my days, in this dark world and wide,
> And that one Talent which is death to hide,
> Lodg'd with me useless, though my Soul more bent
> To serve therewith my Master, and present
> My true account, lest he returning chide :
> Doth God exact day-labour, light deny'd,
> I fondly ask.   But patience, to prevent
> That murmur, soon replies : God doth not need
> Either man's work or his own gifts ; who best
> Bear his mild yoke, they serve him best, his State
> Is Kingly.   Thousands at his bidding Speed
> And post o'er Land and Ocean without rest :
> They also serve who only stand and wait.

Milton did not condescend to the Sonnet ; he wrote it as naturally in the major key as he did his lyrics and epics.

Wordsworth, too.   With his fifty-eight sonnets on the theme of Liberty, and his thirty-seven miscellaneous ones, the form

in his hands was no mere " small lute,"
but (as he wrote of it in connection with
Milton), " the Thing became a trumpet."
It might be said that, for the first time
since Shakespeare, the sonnet really came
into its powerful own. Wordsworth used
it to show all the varying arabesques and
figures that comprise the gamut running
from the fancy up to the imagination.
With it he mused on morality, the obscure
workings of the human spirit, the mutability
of all things. And always the matter was
proper to the Sonnet : a complete, matured
thought fulfilling the prescribed lines—
neither more nor less : adjusted to that
perfection of weight with balance which a
goldsmith achieves scaling his precious
metal. At times light and playful, sunny
with gay conjecturing, as in

Where lies the land to which yon ship must go ?

and then striking, though most delicately,
a slightly deeper note :

With ships the sea was sprinkled far and nigh ;

F

deepening that note, almost imperceptibly, in

> Earth has not anything to show more fair ;

continuing it—with what a sudden and exquisite welling of tenderness !—

> It is a beauteous evening, calm and free ;
> The holy time is quiet as a nun
> Breathless with adoration ; the broad sun
> Is sinking down in its tranquillity ;
> The gentleness of heaven is on the sea :
> Listen ! the mighty being is awake,
> And doth with his eternal motion make
> A sound like thunder everlastingly.
> Dear child ! dear girl ! that walkest with me here—
> If thou appear'st untouch'd by solemn thought,
> Thy nature is not therefore less divine :
> Thou liest " in Abraham's bosom " all the year ;
> And worshipp'st at the temple's inner shrine,
> God being with thee when we know it not.

—then lapsing into despair fiery with indignant protest, in the profoundly beautiful

> The world is too much with us ; late and soon,
> Getting and spending, we lay waste our powers ;
> Little we see in Nature that is ours ;
> We have given our hearts away, a sordid boon !
> This sea that bares her bosom to the moon ;
> The winds that will be howling at all hours

And are up-gather'd now like sleeping flowers ;
For this, for everything, we are out of tune ;
It moves us not.   Great God ! I'd rather be
A pagan suckled in a creed outworn ;
So might I, standing on this pleasant lea,
Have glimpses that would make me less forlorn,
Have sight of Proteus coming from the sea,
Or hear old Triton blow his wreathèd horn.

The high cause of Freedom had in Wordsworth a staunch champion. Incessantly
and jealously he watched over the indi-
vidual's rights, and, whenever needed, his
sonnet-blade flashed out valiantly against
the usurpations of tyranny. " We must
be free or die ! " was his unflinching belief—
holding, as he did, that

There is a bondage which is worse to bear
Than his who breathes, by roof, and floor, and wall,
Pent in, a tyrant's solitary thrall :
'Tis his who walks about in the open air,
One of a nation who, henceforth, must wear
Their fetters in their souls.

I have mentioned above two sonnets
which were obviously penned in white-hot
passion. The first is, as will have been
discerned, Milton's stupendous " Avenge,

O Lord, thy slaughter'd Saints " ; the second is this—Wordsworth's most eloquent and desperate " London, 1802 " :

> Milton ! thou shouldst be living at this hour :
> England hath need of thee : she is a fen
> Of stagnant waters : altar, sword, and pen,
> Fireside, the heroic wealth of hall and bower,
> Have forfeited their ancient English dower
> Of inward happiness.　We are selfish men :
> O raise us up, return to us again ;
> And give us manners, virtue, freedom, power.
> Thy soul was like a star, and dwelt apart :
> Thou hadst a voice whose sound was like the sea ;
> Pure as the naked heavens, majestic, free ;
> So didst thou travel on life's common way,
> In cheerful godliness ; and yet thy heart
> The lowliest duties on itself did lay.

This stern, chiding note was not echoed by Wordsworth's young contemporaries, Shelley and Keats. Shelley wrote one perfect sonnet, and one only. " Ozymandias " is a superb ironic commentary on the vanity of human wishes. The eighth line should be noted as perhaps one of the most masterly examples in the language of imaginative compression :

> I met a traveller from an antique land
> Who said : " Two vast and trunkless legs of stone

Stand in the desert.   Near them on the sand,
Half-sunk, a shattered visage lies, whose frown
And wrinkled lip and sneer of cold command
Tell that its sculptor well those passions read
Which yet survive, stamped on these lifeless things,
The hand that mocked them and the heart that fed.
And on the pedestal these words appear :
' My name is Ozymandias, king of kings ;
Look on my works, ye mighty, and despair ! '
Nothing beside remains.   Round the decay
Of that colossal wreck, boundless and bare,
The lone and level sands stretch far away."

The name of Keats is for ever linked
with the most famous of all sonnets—" On
First Looking Into Chapman's Homer "—
with its incomparable concluding image :

Much have I travell'd in the realms of gold,
And many goodly states and kingdoms seen ;
Round many western islands have I been
Which bards in fealty to Apollo hold.
Oft of one wide expanse had I been told
That deep-brow'd Homer rules as his demesne :
Yet did I never breathe its pure serene
Till I heard Chapman speak out loud and bold :
Then felt I like some watcher of the skies
When a new planet swims into his ken ;
Or like stout Cortez, when with eagle eyes
He stared at the Pacific—and all his men
Look'd at each other with a wild surmise—
Silent, upon a peak in Darien.

It would be impossible to overpraise this wonderful sonnet ; it scales the heights and plants its audacious banner on the very peak of perfection.

The lyrical note known to Shakespeare has returned to the Sonnet. We hear it in Keats's invocation " To Sleep " :

> O soothest Sleep ! if so it please thee, close,
> In midst of this thine hymn, my willing eyes,
> Or wait the amen, ere thy poppy throws
> Around my bed its lulling charities ;

in the concluding two lines that sing themselves into silence :

> Turn the key deftly in the oiled wards,
> And seal the hushed casket of my soul ;

in " The Grasshopper and Cricket " :

> The poetry of earth is never dead :
> When all the birds are faint with the hot sun,
> And hide in cooling trees, a voice will run
> From hedge to hedge about the new-mown mead ;

in " The Elgin Marbles " :

> My spirit is too weak ; mortality
> Weighs heavily on me like unwilling sleep,

And each imagined pinnacle and steep
Of godlike hardship tells me I must die
Like a sick eagle looking at the sky ;

and elsewhere throughout the sonnets, but most especially and completely in the lovely and voluptuous " Last Sonnet " :

Bright Star, would I were steadfast as thou art—
Not in lone splendour hung aloft the night,
And watching, with eternal lids apart,
Like Nature's patient sleepless Eremite,
The moving waters at their priest-like task
Of pure ablution round earth's human shores,
Or gazing on the new soft-fallen mask
Of snow upon the mountains and the moors—
No—yet still steadfast, still unchangeable,
Pillow'd upon my fair love's ripening breast,
To feel for ever its soft fall and swell,
Awake for ever in a sweet unrest,
Still, still to hear her tender-taken breath,
And so live ever—or else swoon to death.

The so-called " Sonnets from the Portuguese " of Elizabeth Barrett Browning were not taken from the Portuguese at all. They were expressions of a love so intimate that it seemed discreet to the poet to give them a disguise—to disown their content,

as it were.   The first of the series is indica-
tive of their quality and tenor :

> I thought once how Theocritus had sung
> Of the sweet years, the dear and wish'd-for years,
> Who each one in a gracious hand appears
> To bear a gift for mortals old or young :
> And, as I mused it in his antique tongue,
> I saw in gradual vision through my tears
> The sweet, sad years, the melancholy years—
> Those of my own life, who by turns had flung
> A shadow across me.   Straightway I was 'ware,
> So weeping, how a mystic Shape did move
> Behind me, and drew me backward by the hair ;
> And a voice said in mastery, while I strove :
> " Guess now who holds thee ? "—" Death," I said.
>   But there
> The silver answer rang—" Not Death, but Love."

They have rather a harsh texture, a certain
verbal and technical maladroitness that
recalls her husband's work. Occasionally
there is the fineness of ineluctability, as,
for instance, when talking of life on earth
with her beloved as

> A place to stand and love in for a day,
> With darkness and the death-hour rounding it ;

but, more usually, she wears the sonnet-
garb with uneasiness.

Rossetti had no such disabilities; the difficulties of the form turned to triumphs under his hand.

The fifty pieces that make up the sequence, " The House of Life," have many splendours to delight in. The brilliant use of metaphor and simile, of telling alliteration and dexterously balanced lines, proclaim the master.

A few examples :

Around the vase of Life at your slow pace
He has not crept, but turned it with his hands,
And all its sides already understands.

* * *

The blushing morn and blushing eve confess
The shame that loads the intolerable day.

* * *

Ah, who shall dare to search through what sad maze
Thenceforth their incommunicable ways
Follow the desultory feet of Death ?

* * *

O lonely night ! art thou not known to me,
A thicket hung with masks of mockery
And watered with the wasteful warmth of tears ?

" Lovesight " is supremely successful, not only for its rapt communication of love adoring, but for its technical accomplishment. The final two lines are matchless, even in his own work :

> When do I see thee, most beloved one ?
> When in the light the spirits of mine eyes
> Before thy face, their altar, solemnize
> The worship of that Love through thee made
>   known ?
> Or when in the dusk hours (we two alone),
> Close-kissed and eloquent of still replies
> Thy twilight-hidden glimmering visage lies,
> And my soul only sees thy soul its own ?
> O love, my love ! if I no more should see
> Thyself, nor on the earth the shadow of thee,
> Nor image of thine eyes in any spring,—
> How then should sound upon Life's darkening slope
> The ground-whirl of the perished leaves of Hope,
> The wind of Death's imperishable wing ?

Rossetti wrote also a number of sonnets on paintings—his own and other artists'. They are no less remarkable than those comprising " The House of Life " sequence. Perhaps the most magical one is that on Giorgione's " Venetian Pastoral "—an astonishing transcription in another medium :

> Water, for anguish of the solstice :—nay,
> But dip the vessel slowly,—nay, but lean
> And hark how at its verge the wave sighs in
> Reluctant.   Hush !   Beyond all depth away :

The heat lies silent at the brink of day ;
Now the hand trails upon the viol-string
That sobs, and the brown faces cease to sing,
Sad with the whole of pleasure. Whither stray
Her eyes now, from whose mouth the slim pipes
    creep
And leave it pouting, while the shadowed grass
Is cool against her naked side ?   Let be :—
Say nothing now unto her—lest she weep,
Nor name this ever.   Be it as it was—
Life touching lips with Immortality.

His sonnets, apart altogether from his
other work, show Rossetti to be a great
individualist among poets.   He stands
alone as indubitably as Shakespeare, Milton
and Wordsworth stand alone.

CHAPTER VII

BEHIND THE VEIL

§

THE mystics among the English poets are a distinguished band. They form an unbroken line from the fourteenth century to the present day. Even the eighteenth century—the Age of Reason—produced its astonishing antidote in William Blake.

The cry of the devout seeker after truth has always been : " O, for a closer walk with God ! " And the mystic poets—properly devout and ever deeply covetous of truth—have recorded their hazardous experiences in attempting that intimate communion. They have sought, by long contemplation and complete abandonment of hampering reason, to surrender themselves utterly to spiritual apprehension of the Deity. The way of the mystical approach is difficult beyond imagination—demanding, not least, abnegation, then annihilation, of selfhood; but it has its ultimate rewards of ecstasy and rapture, correspondingly beyond conjecture.

It may be said that mysticism is a desperate and trusting advance into the unmapped regions of religion :

> O world invisible, we view thee,
> O world intangible, we touch thee,
> O world unknowable, we know thee,
> Inapprehensible, we clutch thee !

At times we find the poetry has meanings that elude—that run before and escape our understanding, as fallen drops of mercury escape the fingers that try to retrieve them. But how is the ineffable to contract into a tiny span of words ? As well seek to put the universe in a thimble. . . .

Here, too, we see in the common use of paradox the measure of language's sheer insufficiency.

But the supreme adventures, if not

related explicitly or definitively, are nevertheless conveyed by quick hints : bright
gleams that penetrate to the attentive spirit
from their hidden source.

§

The mystic way is the way of unflagging
optimism. With infinite faith, step by
painful step, the ascent is made towards
the objective : that glorious, transcendent
absorption into the Deity.

All experience is acceptable : as so many
upward rungs of the ladder of desire.
Nothing can daunt, nor stay, the tremen-
dous effort of the yearning soul.

The boundaries of everyday life dissolve
away ; life and death, no longer separate,
are clasped in each other's arms :

> . . . I die, yet still I do revive ;
>   My living death by dying life is fed ;
> Grace more than nature keeps my heart alive,
>   Whose idle hopes and vain desires are dead.
>
> Not where I breathe, but where I love, I live ;

—so Robert Southwell. And Crashaw echoes him :

> Though still I die, I live again.

But this life that has passed through death, and that is stronger than before—what has been its generative impulse ? In what does union with the Deity consist ? Francis Quarles tells the whole matter :

> I wish a greater knowledge, than t' attain
> The knowledge of MYSELF : A greater Gain
> Than to augment MYSELF : A greater Treasure
> Than to enjoy MYSELF : A greater Pleasure
> Than to content MYSELF ; How slight and vain
> Is all self-knowledge, Pleasure, Treasure, Gain ;
> Unless my better knowledge could retrieve
> My Christ ; unless my better Gain could thrive
> In Christ ; unless my better Wealth grow rich
> In Christ ; unless my better Pleasure pitch
> On Christ. . . .

—and the splendid audacity of the seeking soul is sustained solely by the Divine Love. It is love that is the concomitant of faith ; the Divine Love that causes George Herbert to cry :

> Lord, Thou art mine, and I am Thine ;

and Henry Vaughan to proclaim the first
raptures of the soul recognized and basking :

> O Joys ! Infinite sweetness ! with what flowers,
> And shoots of glory, my soul breaks, and buds !

—and to assert its oneness with the Deity :

> . . . The pious soul by night
> Is like a clouded star, whose beams though said
>   To shed their light
>   Under some cloud,
>   Yet are above,
>   And shine, and move,
>   Beyond that misty shroud.
>   So in my bed,
> That curtain'd grave, though sleep, like ashes, hide
> My lamp, and life, both shall in thee abide.

Thomas Traherne kindles with the same
ecstatic assurance :

> Sweet Infancy !
> O fire of heaven ! O sacred Light
>   How fair and bright,
>   How great am I,
> Whom all the world doth magnify !

> O Heavenly Joy !
> O great and sacred blessedness
>   Which I possess !
>   So great a joy
> Who did into my arms convey ?

From God above
Being sent, the Heavens me enflame :
   To praise His Name
   The stars do move !
The burning sun doth shew His love.

   O how divine
Am I ! To all this sacred wealth,
   This life and health,
   Who raised ? Who mine
Did make the same ? What hand divine ?

(The last three lines of which must surely have been in Blake's mind when he wrote " The Tiger.")

Elsewhere, in celebrating the overwhelming Divine Love, Trahere becomes dithyrambic ; the exclamatory lauds pour forth with vehement unrestraint ; he is drunk with the heavenly " nectar " vouchsafed him :

   O Nectar ! O delicious stream !
O ravishing and only pleasure ! Where
   Shall such another theme
Inspire my tongue with joys or please mine ear !
   Abridgement of delights !
   And Queen of sights !
O mine of rarities ! O Kingdom wide !
O more ! O cause of all ! O glorious Bride !
   O God ! O Bride of God ! O King !
   O soul and crown of everything !

But this is wrestling with the inexpressible for expression, and the victor-poet seems to gain little more than the laurels of incoherence.   He is aware of this, however; his words are far

> Too weak and feeble pictures to express
> The true mysterious depths of Blessedness.

But what else can he do ?   That which is felt so intensely and intimately must be uttered—somehow : that flood of affirmation rising up from the depths of being cannot humanly be kept pent in ; of its own volition it will surge outward seeking the inadequate damming of words.

§

First and last, these experiences are completely exempt from the compulsion of Reason.   The soul is lifted, and (in Isaac Watts's words) " reason lies adoring." John Bannister Tabb dismisses it contemptuously ; it has no part in the means of union with the Godhead :

> . . . Reason and the rays thereof
> Are starlight to the noon of LOVE.

Love and Faith, then, alone are necessary.

> If the sun and moon should doubt,
> They'd immediately go out ;

—thus William Blake. The lesson is obvious : we cease to exist, we are nothing, without faith.

Blake, more than any other of the mystical poets, seems to our eyes to be forever standing "in the streams Of Heaven's bright beams." He wrote much that is exquisite and profound, and much that soars into the rare region of the sublime. Probably his best known poem is the extract from "Milton," in which he so bravely declares his continued aggressiveness in defence of the Ideal :

> Bring me my bow of burning gold !
>   Bring me my arrows of desire !
> Bring me my spear ! O clouds, unfold !
>   Bring me my chariot of fire !
>
> I will not cease from mental fight,
>   Nor shall my sword sleep in my hand,
> Till we have built Jerusalem
>   In England's green and pleasant land.

Much of his work is difficult reading, especially the Prophetic Books. These may be described as " chaos illumined with flashes of lightning." " The Book of Thel " is the simplest of them, as well as the most exquisitely contrived. But all that this extraordinary man wrote is worthy of the closest study.

The activities and desires of the aspiring spirit are as many and varied as the bodies that house them. But always its prime, unflagging desire is to identify itself with the Oneness of All Things, holding with Pope that :

> All are but parts of one tremendous whole,
> Whose body Nature is, and God the soul ;

and with Coleridge that :

> 'Tis the sublime of man,
> Our noontide Majesty, to know ourselves
> Parts and proportions of one wondrous whole ;—

though Coleridge differs importantly from Pope in his emphasis on the very subtle point that

> 'tis God
> Diffused through all, that doth make all one whole.

Tennyson, too, perceived this divine permeation of all things :

> Flower in the crannied wall,
> I pluck you out of the crannies ;—
> Hold you here, root and all, in my hand,
> Little flower—but if I could understand
> What you are, root and all, and all in all,
> I should know what God and man is.

But it was reserved to Francis Thompson—the most important mystical poet since Blake—to expound explicitly the true secret interdependence of the universe. He does it in " The Mistress of Vision " :

> All things by immortal power,
> Near or far,
> Hiddenly
> To each other linked are,
> That thou canst not stir a flower
> Without troubling of a star ;

and again, in " The Kingdom of God " :

> Turn but a stone, and start a wing !

And in all this huge, intricate, consolidated Oneness is immanent the Divine Presence :

> Lo here ! lo there ! ah me, lo everywhere !

This idea of pervasive Divinity is at the core of all Thompson's work. But without doubt it is given its most magnificent expression in " The Hound of Heaven." This poem is one of the glories of latter-day poetry. It is a swiftly-moving piece of sustained grandeur, enriched with all the resources of language : the glittering decorations of simile and metaphor. Its theme is the attempted flight of the Soul from God, who at once pursues it, finally overtakes it, and folds it in His Arms. There are many lines of great beauty, such as :

Across the margent of the world I fled,
    And troubled the gold gateways of the stars,
    Smiting for shelter on their clanged bars ;
    Fretted to dulcet jars
And silvern chatter the pale ports o' the moon.
I said to Dawn : Be sudden—to Eve : Be soon ;
    With thy young skiey blossoms heap me over
    From this tremendous Lover—

and many memorable images, powerful as they are original, such as :

In the rash lustihead of my young powers,
    I shook the pillaring hours
And pulled my life upon me ;

and

> Yea, faileth now even dream
> The dreamer, and the lute the lutanist ;
> Even the linked fantasies, in whose blossomy twist
> I swung the earth a trinket at my wrist,
> Are yielding ;

and

> Ah ! must—
> Designer infinite !—
> Ah ! must Thou char the wood ere Thou canst
>   limn with it ?

and

> Is my gloom, after all,
> Shade of His hand, outstretched caressingly ?

The poem, which must be savoured slowly for its numerous delights, has for conclusion the abiding mystical truth that flight from God is impossible for the soul, since it is on all sides, and for ever, God-encompassed.

To sum up—the singular achievement of the mystical poets lies in their intenser apprehension, their more acutely intuitive knowledge, of the World of the Spirit than their fellow poets.

Thus they have been able to give to Poetry the benefits of an unconjectured enlightenment.

CHAPTER VIII

A TALE TO TELL

§

NARRATIVE poetry has always been by far the most popular kind of poetry. Nor is the reason far to seek. The interest in a *story* is universal and perennial.

Ranging from the ballad to the epic—from the simplest of forms to the most complex—narrative poetry takes the whole of man's experience and imagination for its province. The tale may be of everyday love, romance, adventure ; it may be of the strife of heroes, the exploits of gods.

From the earliest times one of the chief functions of the poet has always been to *entertain,* and this he has done with narrative : celebrations of battle-triumphs ; apologies and consolations for defeats ; recountings of historical happenings ; gay and tender episodes, or grim and fearful imbroglios.

This quality of entertaining has always caught and held the interest of a public that would not have been caught and held by any other kind of poetry ; as, to-day, there are sailors who read " Dauber," and country squires who read " Reynard the Fox," who would not know an ode from a sonnet, nor suffer a glance at either.

The narrative is common enough in poetry ; the epic is rare. What is the difference between them ?

Both tell a tale. It may be said that epic is narrative poetry in its supremest manifestation. Where narrative walks, epic flies. Narrative is a segment of a circle, epic the whole. Narrative stammers, while epic talks with the tongues of men and angels.

§

The formidable length of the chief narrative and epic poems in our language causes them to be little read nowadays. Few beside scholars and students choose to struggle with Chaucer's and Spenser's archaisms. Which is a pity, for the reward is rich.

The " modernity " of Chaucer will be, perhaps, something of a surprise at first, until the reader recollects that human nature has had little time to change in a mere half-millennium.

The " Canterbury Tales " are a cross-section of fourteenth century English life. Their framework is a pilgrimage, from Southwark to St. Thomas's Shrine at Canterbury, by a motley assemblage of people, clerical and lay. The occasion is made a happy holiday as well as a religious observance ; and on the four days' ride tales are told in turn by the pilgrims : tales of chivalry and romance, of noble endurance and low adventure : a range of narrative as great as the diversity of the tellers.

It is all very simple, direct, and fluent, abounding with humour and good spirits.

As genial, but even more fluent in its sustained melody and suave diction, is Spenser's " The Faerie Queene." Indeed, so sinuous, delicious and voluptuous is its music, that a complete reading of the poem affects one in much the same way as would a diet of sweetmeats.

The plan is similar to that of the " Canterbury Tales " : a series of stories told by successive knights present at the annual festival of the faery Queen Gloriana. The poem, planned in twelve books, was only half written when Spenser died. It is a very prolix piece of allegory, for all its many charms : long drawn out and apt to be tedious. Nor is its meaning very clear ; apart from its poor construction, it is best to read the poem for pleasure in the manner in which it is written than for what it is actually about.

These two poems—" The Canterbury Tales " and " The Faerie Queene "—are impressive, if hardly more than entertainments. But Milton's " Paradise Lost " is a spiritual experience. Passing on to it after the other two is like passing on from, say, Humperdinck's " Hansel and Gretel " overture to Bach's Mass in B minor.

The subject of this sublimest of English epics is nothing less than the fall of man and the Divine plan of redemption : an

attempt, in fine, to explain the inexplicable ;
— to " justify the ways of God to men."

Milton was at once a child of the Renais-
sance and of Puritanism. He was a
passionate lover of freedom and beauty.
At the same time, he was remorseless in
seeking to conform all things to the standard
of the Bible, in its Puritan interpretation.
Thus, his was a divided personality : the
poet was ever at war with the Puritan.
We may now say, looking at the poem " fore-
shortened in the tract of time," that to the
poet has gone the eventual victory. The
theology of the poem has ceased to mean
anything to us, but the poetry has lost
nothing in the lapse of years : it is of a
splendour unequalled, and constitutes one
of the final reaches of human genius.

It matters nothing that Classicism and
Biblicism, Hellenism and Hebraism are
incongruously mingled together ; that there
are numerous antinomies and anachron-
isms ; that anthropomorphism is prevalent
throughout, and that, in the end, Satan
inappropriately emerges as the real hero
of the poem. The work triumphs completely over its impossible subject.

Strewn throughout with incomparable lines, with the sublime wedded to the picturesque, the masterpiece is made up of small masterpieces, a few of which may be cited : the assembly of the fallen angels ; Satan's invocation to Light ; the chamber of Eve ; the description of the earthly paradise ; of the morning of the world ; the expulsion from paradise—and all of Satan's discourses.

Here are Adam and Eve asleep :

> These lulled by Nightingales imbraceing slept,
> And on their naked limbs the flourie roof
> Showrd Roses, which the Morn repair'd. Sleep on,
> Blest pair ; and O yet happiest if ye seek
> No happier state, and know to know no more.

And here is evening in paradise :

> Now came still Evening on, and Twilight gray
> Had in her sober Liverie all things clad ;
> Silence accompanied, for Beast and Bird,
> They to thir grassie Couch, these to thir Nests
> Were slunk, all but the wakeful Nightingale ;
> She all night long her amorous descant sung ;
> Silence was pleas'd : now glow'd the Firmament
> With living Saphirs : Hesperus that led
> The starrie Host, rode brightest, till the Moon
> Rising in clouded Majestie, at length
> Apparent Queen unvaild her peerless light,
> And o're the dark her Silver Mantle threw.

§

It seems as though, after Milton, Poetry, awed with her high achievement, stilled her voice awhile. For it cannot be said that, to the critical ear, Thomson, Cowper and Crabbe break the silence ensuing upon the divine psalming of " Paradise Lost."

These didactic, descriptive, bucolic poets have their quiet charm, without doubt, but their work is, in the main, plodding, unambitious and drab.

With Wordsworth and Coleridge, the authentic golden Voice is heard again.

In " The Prelude " Wordsworth tells of his childhood and boyhood : a fine, enthusiastic narrative, kindling with beauty and acute observation. The great achievement of Coleridge is " The Ancient Mariner." In this, a focus is given to all the poet's varied reading and speculation : romantic German ballads, old travels, mystical and occult philosophies, and the resulting poem is compact of imagination and melody : a work of the purest loveliness of word and image and music since Milton.

Though there is implicit a moral in the poem—" love and reverence to all things that God made and loveth " :

> He prayeth well, who loveth well
> Both man and bird and beast.
>
> He prayeth best, who loveth best
> All things both great and small ;—

we need not stumble over it, but take it easily in our stride, for there are by the way such alluring beauties as :

> O Sleep ! it is a gentle thing,
>   Beloved from pole to pole !
> To Mary Queen the praise be given !
> She sent the gentle sleep from Heaven,
>   That slid into my soul ;

and

> And the coming wind did roar more loud,
>   And the sails did sigh like sedge ;
> And the rain poured down from one black cloud ;
>   The Moon was at its edge ;

and

> Sometimes a-dropping from the sky
>   I heard the skylark sing ;

Sometimes all little birds that are,
How they seemed to fill the sea and air
  With their sweet jargoning !

And now 'twas like all instruments,
  Now like a lonely flute ;
And now it is an angel's song,
  That makes the heavens be mute.

Coleridge's fragment of "Christabel" shadows forth a greater poem than even "The Ancient Mariner" ; for into the magic of its imagery and rimes the poet introduces a subtleness of spiritual evil, something of a more profound significance than the Mariner's uncanny experiences. But "Christabel," unfortunately, is a mere fragment. Its descriptive felicity may be exampled by the following night-piece :

The night is chill ; the forest bare ;
Is it the wind that moaneth bleak ?
There is not wind enough in the air
To move away the ringlet curl
From the lovely lady's cheek—
There is not wind enough to twirl
The one red leaf, the last of its clan,
That dances as often as dance it can,
Hanging so light, and hanging so high,
On the topmost twig that looks up at the sky ;

H

and this loving glance at Christabel's chamber :

> The moon shines dim in the open air,
> And not a moonbeam enters here.
> But they without its light can see
> The chamber carved so curiously,
> Carved with figures strange and sweet,
> All made out of the carver's brain,
> For a lady's chamber meet :
> The lamp with twofold silver chain
> Is fastened to an angel's feet.

§

It is difficult to believe to-day that Sir Walter Scott enjoyed a resounding fame as a poet when a young man. Very soon the novelist in him eclipsed the poet, and the loss was not to poetry—the gain was to prose.

He wrote, in " The Lay of the Last Minstrel " and " Marmion," a stark style of verse, direct and most matter-of-fact. Admirably enough, the meaning is always clear—with a hard, sharp clearness. The narratives are always simple, sometimes passionate, but never sensuous. Oddly, he had attempted to model his style upon

Coleridge's admired " Christabel," but the result was as a pygmy wearing a giant's cloak. The very quality that Scott so lamentably lacks—poetic sensuousness—Keats has in full, perhaps over-full, measure. His poetry is like a tropical jungle : lush and thick with verdure and flowers indolent and half-swooning in a hot sun.

" Endymion " has all his virtues and all his vices. It is an immature work, apt to be led on by the exigency of its riming ; but, truly, " every rift is loaded with ore."

The poem begins with one of the very famous lines in our literature :

> A thing of beauty is a joy for ever :
> Its loveliness increases ; it will never
> Pass into nothingness ; but still will keep
> A bower quiet for us, and a sleep
> Full of sweet dreams, and health, and quiet
>   breathing.

This love-tale of the shepherd and the goddess is also the love-tale of the poetic soul and the Absolute Beauty. The hero may be compared with the hero of " The Prelude," and the heroine, indeed, is more like Shelley's Intellectual Beauty than Diana.

"Hyperion" is a great advance on "Endymion." It is at once mature, and displays a masterly power of diction, pictorial felicity, and variety of music. It has some of the ideas present in "Endymion," but they are now applied to the difficult theme of the development of mankind. Keats abandoned the work before finishing it, feeling the style to be beyond his power to maintain, reminding us of Milton's like abandonment of "The Ode on the Nativity."

There are also three shorter narrative poems of Keats to mention : "Lamia," "Isabella," and "The Eve of St. Agnes." This last is the happiest in its scope and achievement. The Spenserian stanza is deftly handled, and the contrast on which the poem is built, between the cold, storm, old age and empty pleasure and noisy enmity of the world outside Madeline's chamber, and the glow, the hush, the rich and dreamy bliss within it, is exquisitely depicted.

There could scarcely be a greater

contrast between any two poets than exists between Keats and Byron. Keats was a romantic of the romantics ; Byron, for all his romantic veneer, was a realist at heart. Byron's poetry is a constant dramatization of himself. He is the hero of " The Giaour," of " The Corsair," of " Lara," of " Don Juan," of " Childe Harold's Pilgrimage."

In these first three tales lies the romantic veneer ; in " Don Juan " and " Childe Harold " the core of the realist, the true Byron. " Don Juan "—full of life, cynicism, swagger—is enthralling reading. And no less so is " Childe Harold." This last, by the way, is responsible for the long-enduring Byronic legend—of the exiled young aristocrat who has sown his wild oats, and who lives to regard the harvest with engaging, but pensive, melancholy.

It is not for magnificence of diction, for grandeur of thought, that we read and re-read Byron, but for his depiction of a real character and description of a real life ; for his unique steeping of every stanza in the strange dyes of his own emotion and sorrow and glamour.

§

After the storm and stress of Byron, Tennyson cannot help but seem mild and domestic But though we somewhat hastily dismiss " Enoch Arden " as a highly sentimental and rather mechanical story, we cannot so hastily, or so easily, dismiss such an outstandingly fine psychological study as " Maud."

The story is narrated in a series of compact lyrics : abounding with loveliness of imagery and description : an acutely analytical account of a sensitive young man facing the difficulties arising not only from the defects of his own character, but also from the workings of a hostile Fate.

We may dismiss the gentle and decorous, competent but undistinguished, " Idylls of the King " (based upon the legend of King Arthur and his Knights of the Round Table) all of them save one, " Morte D'Arthur," —which we will find difficult to praise enough alike for its nobility of language as for its nobility of thought.

And so we come to Browning and Morris, the last of the Victorian writers of epics.

Who nowadays reads " The Ring and the Book " ? Most readers of Browning are content to grapple with his shorter poems, and not try conclusions with his vast and weighty epic. It is not easy reading—this extensive probing of a long-forgotten Roman murder, and its surrounding tragedy. But if we can bring ourselves to the attempt, we shall gain a new appreciation of Browning ; for here, at its highest, he shows his feeling for the power which one soul can wield over another ; his delight in the beauty of innocence ; his deepest meditations on moral wisdom ; and his uttermost indignation against whatever is false, treacherous and cruel.

If " The Ring and the Book " has few readers, it is unlikely that William Morris's " Jason," " The Earthly Paradise " or " Sigurd the Volsung " are any more popular.

Yet these smooth-flowing, picturesque and dexterous, if unwieldy and verbose, epics (for such each is, no less) are as easy

and enjoyable to read as (it must be said)
" The Ring and the Book " is difficult and
demanding of mental effort.

As a rule, easy writing makes hard reading. But Morris wrote as easily and as
naturally as he breathed ; and in his case
the rule does not apply.

Of the three elaborate works, perhaps
" Sigurd the Volsung " has the best chance
of immortality and (for it will never be
widely popular) continuation of its present
" fit audience though few."

CHAPTER IX

THE PRESENT ADVENTURE

§

IT is sometimes maintained that poetry is a dying art ; that the present age, filled with the tolerant scepticism which is the result alike of rapid transport and Freudian analysis, has no place for it. Is this true ? Has the Twilight of the Poets indeed fallen ? If it were true, the poets that are with us would be few in number, and their work decadent.

But a glance at any one of the numerous anthologies of modern verse disposes at once of the pessimistic contention.

Never was there an age so full of poets as the present age, and never was there such diversity of song. Decadence (and then it was only a pose) went out of fashion in the late nineties of last century.

Poetry is not an incongruous, intruding,

anachronistic survival doomed to disappear. It will never pass ; but will be present in the centuries to come as surely as the quenchless aspirations of men's souls.

It is an experience as transfiguring as love. It adds sight to the eyes that already see ; hearing to the ears that already hear ; and perception to the spirit that craves it.

It is a constant renewal : " Behold, I make all things new " ; an enrichment beyond computation.

It would be an impossible task in this brief chapter to detail the aims and achievements of all the poets writing to-day, and to give representative quotations from their work. It must suffice to enumerate several of the most prominent, and to urge the reader not to delay in becoming acquainted with their poetry.

Of the immediate great dead, there are Thomas Hardy, Robert Bridges, Rupert Brooke and James Elroy Flecker. Of the living, there are Mr. A. E. Housman, Sir William Watson, Mr. John Masefield, Mr. Walter de la Mare, Mr. Laurence Binyon, Mr. W. H. Davies, Mr. W. B. Yeats, A. E.,

Mr. James Stephens, Mr. Siegfried Sassoon, Mr. T. S. Eliot and Mr. Edmund Blunden.

There are many more names that might be given, beside, of poets whose work, if minor and of lesser importance, is of decided interest. The two poets who have dominated the last forty years of poetry are Mr. A. E. Housman, with " A Shropshire Lad," and Mr. T. S. Eliot, with " The Waste Land." The former work appeared in 1896, the latter in 1922. " A Shropshire Lad " is a collection of lyrics, exquisite, formal, grave and restrained, which contains a haunting music that fell new on English ears.

The appearance of " The Waste Land " abruptly challenged Mr. Housman's widespread influence, and at once the newest poets changed their allegiance.

" The Waste Land " has been called " a series of inspired chapter-headings " ; but it was a standard of revolt reared in poetry, as defiant as " Ulysses " in prose.

It may be described as a psychoanalytical, quasi-metaphysical poem built on a curious foundation of wide erudition and free association of ideas.

Naturally it has had a host of imitators. Whether it deserves them ; whether poetry has not seemed to take an errant direction since its publication ; whether it is a truly great, or a merely superficial, work, is beside the point.

Its present influence is unquestioned and unquestionable.

Time will see, as Time has always seen, to the survival of that which is worthy to survive, and decently bury that which is deserving of obscurity.

To those who look dubiously or distressfully on the incessant experimenting that is prevalent to-day with new and old forms, new themes, and new words and phrases, in numberless combinations and permutations, it may be pointed out that experiment is the very life-blood of art. Neither stagnation nor decadence can exist while this healthy striving is abroad. Ultimately, in the nature of things, the chaos will subside. We are living in an exciting, exhilarating, restless, questing age, when nothing is taken for granted, on trust, or on hearsay ; we are living in an age—so far as art is concerned—of transition.

We must keep an open mind, and acknowledge sincerity and integrity of purpose when we meet them.

Other ages before ours have been ages of transition. We must remember what Wordsworth wrote, in his Introduction to " Lyrical Ballads," with regard to just this question : the appreciation of a new kind of poetry.

" Readers accustomed to the gaudiness and inane phraseology of many modern writers," he wrote, " if they persist in reading this book to its conclusion, will perhaps frequently have to struggle with feelings of strangeness and awkwardness ; they will look round for poetry, and will be induced to inquire by what species of courtesy these attempts can be permitted to assume that title. It is desirable that such readers, for their own sakes, should not suffer the solitary word ' Poetry,' a word of very disputed meaning, to stand in the way of their gratification ; but that, while they are perusing this book, they should ask themselves if it contains a natural delineation of human passions, human characters and human incidents ;

and if the answer be favourable to the author's wishes, that they should consent to be pleased in spite of that most dreadful enemy to our pleasures—our own pre-established codes of decision."

A very timely warning, this, for the present day; when we are perhaps apt to be too summarily dismissive of work that appears new and strange to us, and not immediately understandable.

The great river of English Poetry flows broadly on, and its tributaries of experimentation feed, not deplete it. Irresistibly it flows, and bears on its breast the dreams and delights of a mighty nation.